My Weekly List

	M	T	W	T	F	S/S
NEED TO						
WANT TO						

TOP 3 PRIORITIES

....

....

....

NOTES

My Weekly List

WEEK OF ....

	M	T	W	T	F	S/S
NEED TO						
WANT TO						

TOP 3 PRIORITIES

....

....

....

NOTES

My Weekly List

WEEK OF ....

	M	T	W	T	F	S/S
NEED TO						
WANT TO						

TOP 3 PRIORITIES

....

....

....

NOTES

My Weekly List

WEEK OF ....

	M	T	W	T	F	S / S
NEED TO						
WANT TO						

TOP 3 PRIORITIES

....

....

....

NOTES

My Weekly List

WEEK OF ....

	M	T	W	T	F	S / S
NEED TO						
WANT TO						

TOP 3 PRIORITIES

....

....

....

NOTES

My Weekly List

WEEK OF ....

	M	T	W	T	F	S / S
NEED TO						
WANT TO						

TOP 3 PRIORITIES

....

....

....

NOTES

My Weekly List

WEEK OF ....

	M	T	W	T	F	S / S
NEED TO						
WANT TO						

TOP 3 PRIORITIES

....

....

....

NOTES

My Weekly List

WEEK OF ....

	M	T	W	T	F	S/S
NEED TO						
WANT TO						

TOP 3 PRIORITIES

....

....

....

NOTES

My Weekly List

WEEK OF ....

	M	T	W	T	F	S / S
NEED TO						
WANT TO						

TOP 3 PRIORITIES

....

....

....

NOTES

My Weekly List

WEEK OF ....

	M	T	W	T	F	S / S
NEED TO						
WANT TO						

TOP 3 PRIORITIES

....

....

....

NOTES

WEEK OF ....

My Weekly List

	M	T	W	T	F	S/S
NEED TO						
WANT TO						

TOP 3 PRIORITIES

....

....

....

NOTES

My Weekly List

WEEK OF ....

	M	T	W	T	F	S / S
NEED TO						
WANT TO						

TOP 3 PRIORITIES

....

....

....

NOTES

My Weekly List

WEEK OF ....

	M	T	W	T	F	S / S
NEED TO						
WANT TO						

TOP 3 PRIORITIES

....

....

....

NOTES

My Weekly List

WEEK OF . . . .

	M	T	W	T	F	S/S
NEED TO						
WANT TO						

TOP 3 PRIORITIES

. . . .

. . . .

. . . .

NOTES

My Weekly List

WEEK OF ....

M	T	W	T	F	S / S

NEED TO

WANT TO

TOP 3 PRIORITIES

....

....

....

NOTES

My Weekly List

WEEK OF ....

M	T	W	T	F	S / S

NEED TO

WANT TO

TOP 3 PRIORITIES

....

....

....

NOTES

My Weekly List

WEEK OF ....

	M	T	W	T	F	S / S
NEED TO						
WANT TO						

TOP 3 PRIORITIES

....

....

....

NOTES

My Weekly List

WEEK OF ....

	M	T	W	T	F	S / S
NEED TO						
WANT TO						

TOP 3 PRIORITIES

....

....

....

NOTES

My Weekly List

WEEK OF ....

	M	T	W	T	F	S / S
NEED TO						
WANT TO						

TOP 3 PRIORITIES

....

....

....

NOTES

My Weekly List

WEEK OF ....

	M	T	W	T	F	S / S
NEED TO						
WANT TO						

TOP 3 PRIORITIES

....

....

....

NOTES

My Weekly List

WEEK OF ....

M	T	W	T	F	S / S

NEED TO

WANT TO

TOP 3 PRIORITIES

....

....

....

NOTES

My Weekly List

WEEK OF ....

M	T	W	T	F	S/S
NEED TO					
WANT TO					

TOP 3 PRIORITIES

....

....

....

NOTES

My Weekly List

WEEK OF ....

	M	T	W	T	F	S / S
NEED TO						
WANT TO						

TOP 3 PRIORITIES

....

....

....

NOTES

My Weekly List

WEEK OF ....

	M	T	W	T	F	S / S
NEED TO						
WANT TO						

TOP 3 PRIORITIES

....

....

....

NOTES

My Weekly List

WEEK OF ....

	M	T	W	T	F	S/S
NEED TO						
WANT TO						

TOP 3 PRIORITIES

....

....

....

NOTES

My Weekly List

WEEK OF ....

M	T	W	T	F	S/S

NEED TO

WANT TO

TOP 3 PRIORITIES

....

....

....

NOTES

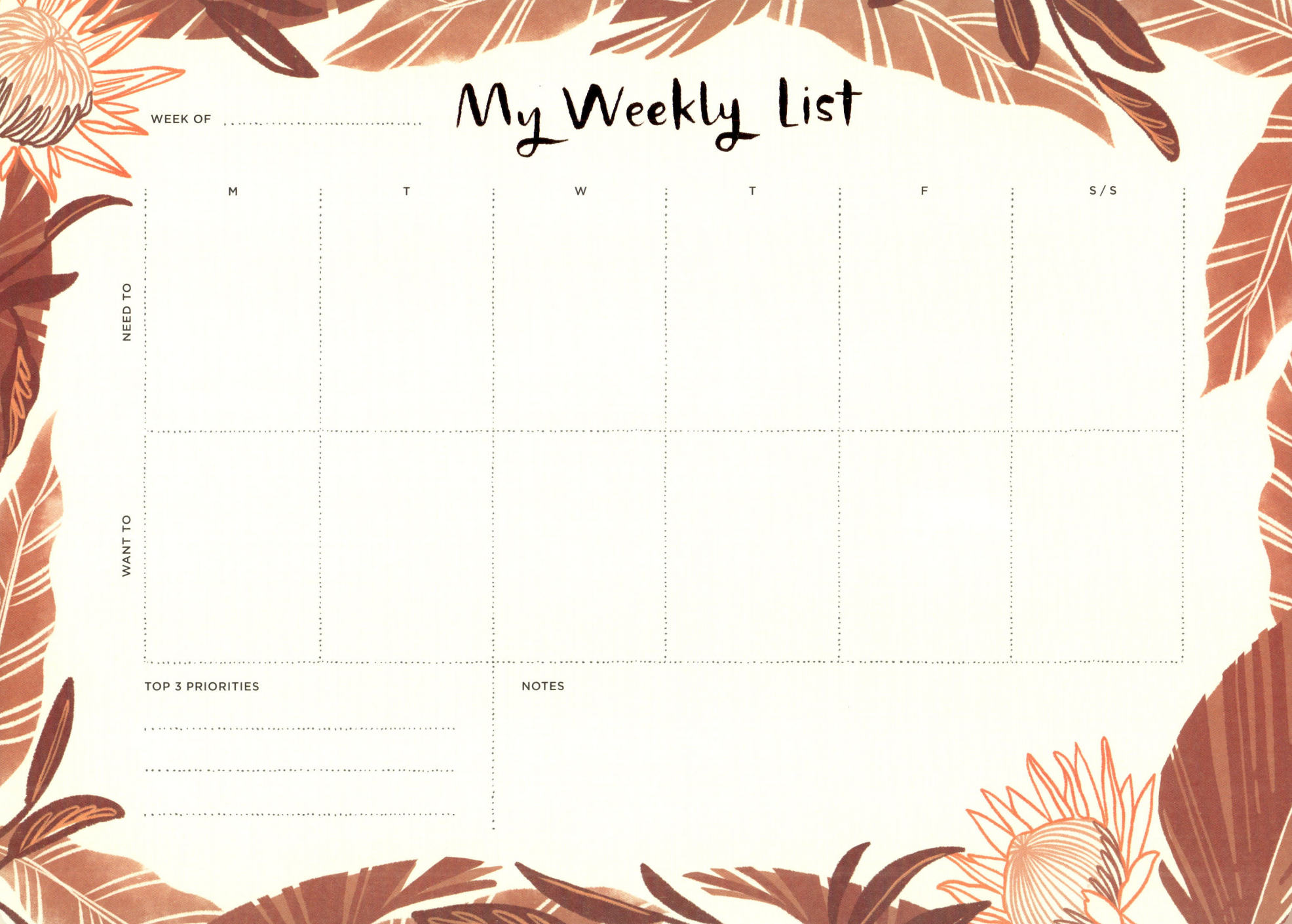

My Weekly List

WEEK OF ....

	M	T	W	T	F	S / S
NEED TO						
WANT TO						

TOP 3 PRIORITIES

....

....

....

NOTES

My Weekly List

	M	T	W	T	F	S / S
NEED TO						
WANT TO						

TOP 3 PRIORITIES

....

....

....

NOTES

My Weekly List

WEEK OF ....

	M	T	W	T	F	S/S
NEED TO						
WANT TO						

TOP 3 PRIORITIES

....

....

....

NOTES

My Weekly List

WEEK OF ....

	M	T	W	T	F	S/S
NEED TO						
WANT TO						

TOP 3 PRIORITIES

....

....

....

NOTES

My Weekly List

WEEK OF ....

	M	T	W	T	F	S / S
NEED TO						
WANT TO						

TOP 3 PRIORITIES

....

....

....

NOTES

My Weekly List

WEEK OF ....

	M	T	W	T	F	S/S
NEED TO						
WANT TO						

TOP 3 PRIORITIES

....

....

....

NOTES

My Weekly List

M	T	W	T	F	S/S

NEED TO

WANT TO

TOP 3 PRIORITIES

....

....

....

NOTES

My Weekly List

WEEK OF ....

	M	T	W	T	F	S/S
NEED TO						
WANT TO						

TOP 3 PRIORITIES

....

....

....

NOTES

My Weekly List

WEEK OF ....

	M	T	W	T	F	S/S
NEED TO						
WANT TO						

TOP 3 PRIORITIES

....

....

....

NOTES

My Weekly List

WEEK OF ....

	M	T	W	T	F	S / S
NEED TO						
WANT TO						

TOP 3 PRIORITIES

....

....

....

NOTES

My Weekly List

WEEK OF ....

	M	T	W	T	F	S / S
NEED TO						
WANT TO						

TOP 3 PRIORITIES

....

....

....

NOTES

My Weekly List

WEEK OF ....

M	T	W	T	F	S / S

NEED TO

WANT TO

TOP 3 PRIORITIES

....

....

....

NOTES

My Weekly List

WEEK OF ....

	M	T	W	T	F	S / S
NEED TO						
WANT TO						

TOP 3 PRIORITIES

....

....

....

NOTES

My Weekly List

WEEK OF ....

	M	T	W	T	F	S/S
NEED TO						
WANT TO						

TOP 3 PRIORITIES

....

....

....

NOTES

My Weekly List

WEEK OF ....

M	T	W	T	F	S/S

NEED TO

WANT TO

TOP 3 PRIORITIES

....

....

....

NOTES

My Weekly List

WEEK OF ....

	M	T	W	T	F	S / S
NEED TO						
WANT TO						

TOP 3 PRIORITIES

....

....

....

NOTES

My Weekly List

WEEK OF ....

	M	T	W	T	F	S/S
NEED TO						
WANT TO						

TOP 3 PRIORITIES

....

....

....

NOTES

My Weekly List

WEEK OF ....

	M	T	W	T	F	S / S
NEED TO						
WANT TO						

TOP 3 PRIORITIES

....

....

....

NOTES

My Weekly List

WEEK OF ....

	M	T	W	T	F	S/S
NEED TO						
WANT TO						

TOP 3 PRIORITIES

....

....

....

NOTES

My Weekly List

WEEK OF ....

M	T	W	T	F	S/S

NEED TO

WANT TO

TOP 3 PRIORITIES

....

....

....

NOTES

My Weekly List

WEEK OF ....

M	T	W	T	F	S/S

NEED TO

WANT TO

TOP 3 PRIORITIES

....

....

....

NOTES

My Weekly List

WEEK OF ....

	M	T	W	T	F	S / S
NEED TO						
WANT TO						

TOP 3 PRIORITIES

....

....

....

NOTES

My Weekly List

WEEK OF ....

	M	T	W	T	F	S / S

NEED TO

WANT TO

TOP 3 PRIORITIES

....

....

....

NOTES

My Weekly List

WEEK OF ....

	M	T	W	T	F	S / S

NEED TO

WANT TO

TOP 3 PRIORITIES

....

....

....

NOTES

My Weekly List

WEEK OF ....

	M	T	W	T	F	S/S
NEED TO						
WANT TO						

TOP 3 PRIORITIES

....

....

....

NOTES